Behold HE IS RISEN
A SCRIPTURAL ACCOUNT OF THE
ATONEMENT & RESURRECTION OF
JESUS CHRIST

COMPILATION BY:

NATALIE ELLIS & JONATHAN ELLIS

Scriptural passages in this book are quoted from the Holy Bible, the Book of Mormon and the Pearl of Great Price.
Biblical passages are from The King James translations.
Book of Mormon passages are quoted from the standard text of The Book of Mormon: Another Testament of Jesus Christ.
The selection, arrangement, and presentation of these scriptures, as well as all illustrations and design elements, are original to this work.

This book is intended for devotional, educational, and family reading purposes.
No commentary, paraphrasing, or interpretation has been added to the scriptural text.

First Edition
Printed in the United States of America
ISBN: 978-1-969494-07-9

Behold HE IS RISEN

The Premortal World

Abraham 3:22
Now the Lord had shown unto me, Abraham, the intelligences that were organized before the world was; and among all these there were many of the noble and great ones;

Abraham 3:24
And there stood one among them that was like unto God, and he said unto those who were with him: We will go down, for there is space there, and we will take of these materials, and we will make an earth whereon these may dwell;

Abraham 3:25
And we will prove them herewith, to see if they will do all things whatsoever the Lord their God shall command them;

Abraham 3:27
And the Lord said: Whom shall I send? And one answered like unto the Son of Man: Here am I, send me. And another answered and said: Here am I, send me. And the Lord said: I will send the first.

The Premortal World

Moses 4:1
And I, the Lord God, spake unto Moses, saying: That Satan, whom thou has commanded in the name of mine Only Begotten, is the same which was from the beginning, and he came before me, saying - Behold, here am I, send me, I will be thy son, and I will redeem all mankind, that one soul shall not be lost, and surely I will do it; wherefore give me thine honor.

Moses 4:2
But, behold, my Beloved Son, which was my Beloved and Chosen from the beginning, said unto me - Father, thy will be done, and the glory be thine forever.

Abraham 4:1
And then the Lord said: Let us go down. And they went down at the beginning, and they, that is the Gods, organized and formed the heavens and the earth.

...After the creation ...

Moses 5:9
And in that day the Holy Ghost fell upon Adam, which beareth record of the Father and the Son, saying: I am the Only Begotten of the Father from the beginning, henceforth and forever, that as thou hast fallen thou mayest be redeemed, and all mankind, even as many as will.

Moses 1:39
For behold, this is my work and my glory - to bring to pass the immortality and eternal life of man.

PROPHECIES OF THE MESSIAH

740-700 BC - Israel

Isaiah 53:4
Surely he hath borne our griefs, and carried our sorrows: yet we did esteem him stricken, smitten of God, and afflicted.

Isaiah 53:5
But he was wounded for our transgressions, he was bruised for our iniquities: the chastisement of our peace was upon him: and with his stripes we are healed.

Isaiah 53:6
All we like sheep have gone astray; we have turned every one to his own way; and the LORD hath laid on him the iniquity of us all.

PROPHECIES OF THE MESSIAH

Mosiah 3:5
For behold, the time cometh, and is not far distant, that with power, the Lord Omnipotent who reigneth, who was, and is from all eternity to all eternity, shall come down from heaven among the children of men, and shall dwell in a tabernacle of clay, and shall go forth amongst men, working mighty miracles, such as healing the sick, raising the dead, causing the lame to walk, the blind to receive their sight, and the deaf to hear, and curing all manner of diseases.

Mosiah 3:6
And he shall cast out devils, or the evil spirits which dwell in the hearts of the children of men.

Mosiah 3:7
And lo, he shall suffer temptations, and pain of body, hunger, thirst, and fatigue, even more than man can suffer, except it be unto death; for behold, blood cometh from every pore, so great shall be his anguish for the wickedness and the abominations of his people.

Mosiah 3:8
And he shall be called Jesus Christ, the Son of God, the Father of heaven and earth, the Creator of all things from the beginning; and his mother shall be called Mary.

PROPHECIES OF THE MESSIAH

124 BC - Americas

Mosiah 3:9
And lo, he cometh unto his own, that salvation might come unto the children of men even through faith on his name; and even after all this they shall consider him a man, and say that he hath a devil, and shall scourge him, and shall crucify him.

Mosiah 3:10
And he shall rise the third day from the dead; and behold, he standeth to judge the world; and behold, all these things are done that a righteous judgment might come upon the children of men.

PROPHECIES OF THE MESSIAH

Alma 7:11

And he shall go forth, suffering pains and afflictions and temptations of every kind; and this that the word might be fulfilled which saith he will take upon him the pains and the sicknesses of his people.

Alma 7:12

And he will take upon him death, that he may loose the bands of death which bind his people; and he will take upon him their infirmities, that his bowels may be filled with mercy, according to the flesh, that he may know according to the flesh how to succor his people according to their infirmities.

Alma 7:13

Now the Spirit knoweth all things; nevertheless the Son of God suffereth according to the flesh that he might take upon him the sins of his people, that he might blot out their transgressions according to the power of his deliverance; and now behold, this is the testimony which is in me.

HIS LIFE AND MINISTRY

Mark 1:9
And it came to pass in those days, that Jesus came from Nazareth of Galilee, and was baptized of John in Jordan.

Mark 1:10
And straightway coming up out of the water, he saw the heavens opened, and the Spirit like a dove descending upon him:

Mark 1:11
And there came a voice from heaven, saying, Thou art my beloved Son, in whom I am well pleased.

———————————————

Matthew 4:23
And Jesus went about all Galilee, teaching in their synagogues, and preaching the gospel of the kingdom, and healing all manner of sickness and all manner of disease among the people.

John 9:1
And as Jesus passed by, he saw a man which was blind from his birth.

John 9:6
When he had thus spoken, he spat on the ground, and made clay of the spittle, and he anointed the eyes of the blind man with the clay,

John 9:7
And said unto him, Go, wash in the pool of Siloam, (which is by interpretation, Sent.) He went his way therefore, and washed, and came seeing.

His Life and Ministry

Matthew 14:14
And Jesus went forth, and saw a great multitude, and was moved with compassion toward them, and he healed their sick.

Matthew 14:19
And he commanded the multitude to sit down on the grass, and took the five loaves, and the two fishes, and looking up to heaven, he blessed, and brake, and gave the loaves to his disciples, and the disciples to the multitude.

Matthew 14:20
And they did all eat, and were filled: and they took up of the fragments that remained twelve baskets full.

Matthew 14:21
And they that had eaten were about five thousand men, beside women and children.

Mark 4:37
And there arose a great storm of wind, and the waves beat into the ship, so that it was now full.

Mark 4:39
And he arose, and rebuked the wind, and said unto the sea, Peace, be still. And the wind ceased, and there was a great calm.

Matthew 9:2
And, behold, they brought to him a man sick of the palsy, lying on a bed: and Jesus seeing their faith said unto the sick of the palsy; Son, be of good cheer; thy sins be forgiven thee.

Matthew 9:6
But that ye may know that the Son of man hath power on earth to forgive sins, (then saith he to the sick of the palsy,) Arise, take up thy bed, and go unto thine house.

Matthew 9:7
And he arose, and departed to his house.

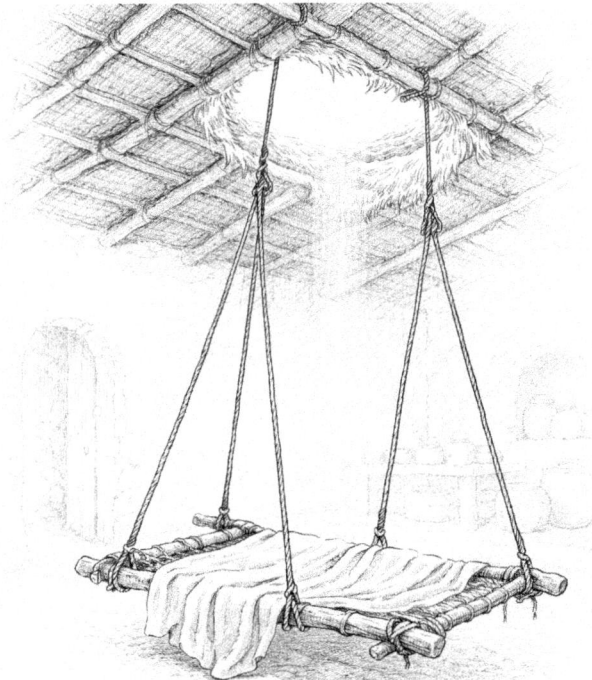

His Life and Ministry

John 11:14
Then said Jesus unto them plainly, Lazarus is dead.

John 11:17
Then when Jesus came, he found that he had lain in the grave four days already.

John 11:21
Then said Martha unto Jesus, Lord, if thou hadst been here, my brother had not died.

John 11:23
Jesus saith unto her, Thy brother shall rise again.

John 11:25
Jesus said unto her, I am the resurrection, and the life: he that believeth in me, though he were dead, yet shall he live:

John 11:26
And whosoever liveth and believeth in me shall never die. Believest thou this?

THE TRIUMPHAL ENTRY

Matthew 21:1
And when they drew nigh unto Jerusalem, and were come to Bethphage, unto the mount of Olives, then sent Jesus two disciples,

Mark 11:2
And saith unto them, Go your way into the village over against you: and as soon as ye be entered into it, ye shall find a colt tied, whereon never man sat; loose him, and bring him.

Mark 11:7
And they brought the colt to Jesus, and cast their garments on him; and he sat upon him.

Matthew 21:8
And a very great multitude spread their garments in the way; others cut down branches from the trees, and strawed them in the way.

Matthew 21:9
And the multitudes that went before, and that followed, cried, saying, Hosanna to the Son of David: Blessed is he that cometh in the name of the Lord; Hosanna in the highest.

Matthew 21:10
And when he was come into Jerusalem, all the city was moved, saying, Who is this?

Matthew 21:11
And the multitude said, This is Jesus the prophet of Nazareth of Galilee.

THE LAST SUPPER

Luke 22:1
Now the feast of unleavened bread drew nigh, which is called the Passover.

Luke 22:14
And when the hour was come, he sat down, and the twelve apostles with him.

John 13:4
He riseth from supper, and laid aside his garments; and took a towel, and girded himself.

John 13:5
After that he poureth water into a basin, and began to wash the disciples' feet, and to wipe them with the towel wherewith he was girded.

Luke 22:15
And he said unto them, With desire I have desired to eat this passover with you before I suffer:

Mark 14:18
And as they sat and did eat, Jesus said, Verily I say unto you, One of you which eateth with me shall betray me.

Mark 14:19
And they began to be sorrowful, and to say unto him one by one, Is it I? and another said, Is it I?

THE LAST SUPPER

Luke 22:19
And he took bread, and gave thanks, and brake it, and
gave unto them, saying, This is my body which is given
for you: this do in remembrance of me.

Luke 22:20
Likewise also the cup after supper, saying, This cup is the
new testament in my blood, which is shed for you.

Matthew 26:30
And when they had sung an hymn, they went out into the
mount of Olives.

GETHSEMANE

Matthew 26:14
Then one of the twelve, called Judas Iscariot, went unto
the chief priests,

Matthew 26:15
And said unto them, What will ye give me, and I will
deliver him unto you? And they covenanted with him for
thirty pieces of silver.

Matthew 26:16
And from that time he sought opportunity to betray him.

Luke 22:39
And he came out, and went, as he was wont, to the mount
of Olives; and his disciples also followed him.

Matthew 26:36
Then cometh Jesus with them unto a place called
Gethsemane, and saith unto the disciples, Sit ye here,
while I go and pray yonder.

Matthew 26:38
Then saith he unto them, My soul is exceeding sorrowful,
even unto death: tarry ye here, and watch with me.

Luke 22:41
And he was withdrawn from them about a stone's cast,
and kneeled down, and prayed.

GETHSEMANE

Matthew 26:39
And he went a little further, and fell on his face, and prayed, saying, O my Father, if it be possible, let this cup pass from me: nevertheless not as I will, but as thou wilt.

Matthew 26:42
He went away again the second time, and prayed, saying, O my Father, if this cup may not pass away from me, except I drink it, thy will be done.

Matthew 26:44
And he left them, and went away again, and prayed the third time, saying the same words.

Luke 22:43
And there appeared an angel unto him from heaven, strengthening him.

Luke 22:44
And being in an agony he prayed more earnestly: and his sweat was as it were great drops of blood falling down to the ground.

Matthew 26:45
Then cometh he to his disciples, and saith unto them, Sleep on now, and take your rest: behold, the hour is at hand, and the Son of man is betrayed into the hands of sinners.

THE CRUCIFIXION

Luke 22:47

And while he yet spake, behold a multitude, and he that was called Judas, one of the twelve, went before them, and drew near unto Jesus to kiss him.

Matthew 26:48

Now he that betrayed him gave them a sign, saying, Whomsoever I shall kiss, that same is he: hold him fast.

Matthew 26:49

And forthwith he came to Jesus, and said, Hail, master; and kissed him.

Matthew 26:50

And Jesus said unto him, Friend, wherefore art thou come? Then came they, and laid hands on Jesus, and took him.

Luke 22:50

And one of them smote the servant of the high priest, and cut off his right ear.

Luke 22:51

And Jesus answered and said, Suffer ye thus far. And he touched his ear, and healed him.

Luke 22:54

Then took they him, and led him, and brought him into the high priest's house. And Peter followed afar off.

THE CRUCIFIXION

Matthew 26:59
Now the chief priests, and elders, and all the council, sought false witness against Jesus, to put him to death;

Matthew 26:66
What think ye? They answered and said, He is guilty of death.

Matthew 26:67
Then did they spit in his face, and buffeted him; and others smote him with the palms of their hands,

Matthew 27:2
And when they had bound him, they led him away, and delivered him to Pontius Pilate the governor.

Matthew 27:15
Now at that feast the governor was wont to release unto the people a prisoner, whom they would.

Matthew 27:17
Therefore when they were gathered together, Pilate said unto them, Whom will ye that I release unto you? Barabbas, or Jesus which is called Christ?

THE CRUCIFIXION

Matthew 27:21
The governor answered and said unto them, Whether of the twain will ye that I release unto you? They said, Barabbas.

Matthew 27:22
Pilate saith unto them, What shall I do then with Jesus which is called Christ? They all say unto him, Let him be crucified.

Matthew 27:24
When Pilate saw that he could prevail nothing, but that rather a tumult was made, he took water, and washed his hands before the multitude, saying, I am innocent of the blood of this just person: see ye to it.

Matthew 27:26
Then released he Barabbas unto them: and when he had scourged Jesus, he delivered him to be crucified.

Matthew 27:28
And they stripped him, and put on him a scarlet robe.

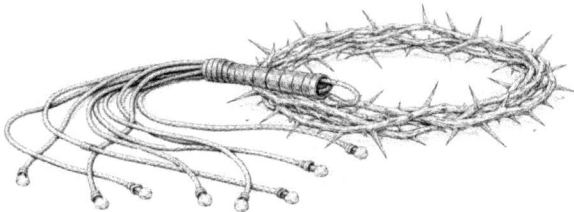

THE CRUCIFIXION

Matthew 27:29
And when they had plaited a crown of thorns, they put it upon his head, and a reed in his right hand: and they bowed the knee before him, and mocked him, saying, Hail, King of the Jews!

Matthew 27:30
And they spit upon him, and took the reed, and smote him on the head.

Matthew 27:31
And after that they had mocked him, they took the robe off from him, and put his own raiment on him, and led him away to crucify him.

Matthew 27:33
And when they were come unto a place called Golgotha, that is to say, a place of a skull,

Matthew 27:34
They gave him vinegar to drink mingled with gall: and when he had tasted thereof, he would not drink.

Matthew 27:35
And they crucified him, and parted his garments, casting lots: that it might be fulfilled which was spoken by the prophet, They parted my garments among them, and upon my vesture did they cast lots.

THE CRUCIFIXION

Luke 23:34
Then said Jesus, Father, forgive them; for they know not
what they do. And they parted his raiment, and cast lots.

Matthew 27:37
And set up over his head his accusation written, THIS IS
JESUS THE KING OF THE JEWS.

Matthew 27:45
Now from the sixth hour there was darkness over all the
land unto the ninth hour.

Matthew 27:46
And about the ninth hour Jesus cried with a loud voice,
saying, Eli, Eli, lama sabachthani? that is to say, My God,
my God, why hast thou forsaken me?

Luke 23:46
And when Jesus had cried with a loud voice, he said,
Father, into thy hands I commend my spirit: and having
said thus, he gave up the ghost.

ישוע מל הנצרי מלך היהודים
ΙΗΣΟΥΣ Ο ΝΑΖΩΡΑΙΟΣ Ο ΒΑΣΙΛΕΥΣ ΤΩΝ ΙΟΥΛΛΙΩΝ
IESUS NAZARENVS REX IVDAEORUM

THE CRUCIFIXION

3 Nephi 8:3
And the people began to look with great earnestness for the sign which had been given by the prophet Samuel, the Lamanite, yea, for the time that there should be darkness for the space of three days over the face of the land.

3 Nephi 8:5
And it came to pass in the thirty and fourth year, in the first month, on the fourth day of the month, there arose a great storm, such an one as never had been known in all the land.

3 Nephi 8:11
And there was a great and terrible destruction in the land southward.

3 Nephi 8:12
But behold, there was a more great and terrible destruction in the land northward; for behold, the whole face of the land was changed, because of the tempest and the whirlwinds, and the thunderings and the lightnings, and the exceedingly great quaking of the whole earth;

3 Nephi 8:17
And thus the face of the whole earth became deformed, because of the tempests, and the thunderings, and the lightnings, and the quaking of the earth.

THE CRUCIFIXION

3 Nephi 8:20

And it came to pass that there was thick darkness upon all the face of the land, insomuch that the inhabitants thereof who had not fallen could feel the vapor of darkness;

3 Nephi 8:23

And it came to pass that it did last for the space of three days that there was no light seen; and there was great mourning and howling and weeping among all the people continually; yea, great were the groanings of the people, because of the darkness and the great destruction which had come upon them.

3 Nephi 9:1

And it came to pass that there was a voice heard among all the inhabitants of the earth, upon all the face of this land, crying:

3 Nephi 9:15

Behold, I am Jesus Christ the Son of God. I created the heavens and the earth, and all things that in them are. I was with the Father from the beginning. I am in the Father, and the Father in me; and in me hath the Father glorified his name.

The Crucifixion

3 Nephi 9:16

I came unto my own, and my own received me not. And
the scriptures concerning my coming are fulfilled.

3 Nephi 9:17

And as many as have received me, to them have I given to
become the sons of God; and even so will I to as many as
shall believe on my name, for behold, by me redemption
cometh, and in me is the law of Moses fulfilled.

3 Nephi 9:18

I am the light and the life of the world. I am Alpha and
Omega, the beginning and the end.

3 Nephi 9:22

Therefore, whoso repenteth and cometh unto me as a
little child, him will I receive, for of such is the kingdom
of God. Behold, for such I have laid down my life, and
have taken it up again; therefore repent, and come unto
me ye ends of the earth, and be saved.

3 Nephi 10:1

And now behold, it came to pass that all the people of the
land did hear these sayings, and did witness of it. And
after these sayings there was silence in the land for the
space of many hours;

The Tomb

Matthew 27:57
When the even was come, there came a rich man of Arimathaea, named Joseph, who also himself was Jesus' disciple:

Matthew 27:58
He went to Pilate, and begged the body of Jesus. Then Pilate commanded the body to be delivered.

John 19:40
Then took they the body of Jesus, and wound it in linen clothes with the spices, as the manner of the Jews is to bury.

Matthew 27:60
And laid it in his own new tomb, which he had hewn out in the rock: and he rolled a great stone to the door of the sepulchre, and departed.

Pilate sets a watch

Matthew 27:65
Pilate said unto them, Ye have a watch: go your way, make it as sure as ye can.

Matthew 27:66
So they went, and made the sepulchre sure, sealing the stone, and setting a watch.

THE RESURRECTION

Matthew 28:1

In the end of the sabbath, as it began to dawn toward the
first day of the week, came Mary Magdalene and the
other Mary to see the sepulchre.

Mark 16:3

And they said among themselves, Who shall roll us away
the stone from the door of the sepulchre?

Mark 16:4

And when they looked, they saw that the stone was rolled
away: for it was very great.

Mark 16:5

And entering into the sepulchre, they saw a young man
sitting on the right side, clothed in a long white garment;
and they were affrighted.

Matthew 28:5

And the angel answered and said unto the women, Fear
not ye: for I know that ye seek Jesus, which was crucified.

Matthew 28:6

He is not here: for he is risen, as he said. Come, see the
place where the Lord lay.

Mark 16:7

But go your way, tell his disciples and Peter that he goeth
before you into Galilee: there shall ye see him, as he said
unto you.

THE RESURRECTION

John 20:2
Then she runneth, and cometh to Simon Peter, and to the other disciple, whom Jesus loved, and saith unto them, They have taken away the Lord out of the sepulchre, and we know not where they have laid him.

Luke 24:12
Then arose Peter, and ran unto the sepulchre; and stooping down, he beheld the linen clothes laid by themselves, and departed, wondering in himself at that which was come to pass.

John 20:11
But Mary stood without at the sepulchre weeping: and as she wept, she stooped down, and looked into the sepulchre,

John 20:12
And seeth two angels in white sitting, the one at the head, and the other at the feet, where the body of Jesus had lain.

The Resurrection

John 20:13
And they say unto her, Woman, why weepest thou? She saith unto them, Because they have taken away my Lord, and I know not where they have laid him.

John 20:14
And when she had thus said, she turned herself back, and saw Jesus standing, and knew not that it was Jesus.

John 20:15
Jesus saith unto her, Woman, why weepest thou? whom seekest thou? She, supposing him to be the gardener, saith unto him, Sir, if thou have borne him hence, tell me where thou hast laid him, and I will take him away.

John 20:16
Jesus saith unto her, Mary. She turned herself, and saith unto him, Rabboni; which is to say, Master.

John 20:17
Jesus saith unto her, Touch me not; for I am not yet ascended to my Father: but go to my brethren, and say unto them, I ascend unto my Father, and your Father; and to my God, and your God.

John 20:18
Mary Magdalene came and told the disciples that she had seen the Lord, and that he had spoken these things unto her.

The Resurrection

Luke 24:13
And, behold, two of them went that same day to a village called Emmaus, which was from Jerusalem about threescore furlongs.

Luke 24:14
And they talked together of all these things which had happened.

Luke 24:15
And it came to pass, that, while they communed together and reasoned, Jesus himself drew near, and went with them.

Luke 24:16
But their eyes were holden that they should not know him.

Luke 24:29
But they constrained him, saying, Abide with us: for it is toward evening, and the day is far spent. And he went in to tarry with them.

Luke 24:30
And it came to pass, as he sat at meat with them, he took bread, and blessed it, and brake, and gave to them.

Luke 24:31
And their eyes were opened, and they knew him; and he vanished out of their sight.

THE RESURRECTION

John 20:19
Then the same day at evening, being the first day of the
week, when the doors were shut where the disciples were
assembled for fear of the Jews, came Jesus and stood in
the midst, and saith unto them, Peace be unto you.

Luke 24:39
Behold my hands and my feet, that it is I myself: handle
me, and see; for a spirit hath not flesh and bones, as ye see
me have.

John 20:20
And when he had so said, he shewed unto them his hands
and his side. Then were the disciples glad, when they saw
the Lord.

John 20:21
Then said Jesus to them again, Peace be unto you: as my
Father hath sent me, even so send I you.

Luke 24:48
And ye are witnesses of these things.

A Risen Lord To All The World

3 Nephi 11:1
And now it came to pass that there were a great
multitude gathered together, of the people of Nephi,
round about the temple which was in the land Bountiful;
and they were marveling and wondering one with
another, and were showing one to another the great and
marvelous change which had taken place.

3 Nephi 11:2
And they were also conversing about this Jesus Christ, of
whom the sign had been given concerning his death.

3 Nephi 11:3
And it came to pass that while they were thus conversing
one with another, they heard a voice as if it came out of
heaven; and they cast their eyes round about, for they
understood not the voice which they heard; and it was
not a harsh voice, neither was it a loud voice;
nevertheless, and notwithstanding it being a small voice it
did pierce them that did hear to the center, insomuch
that there was no part of their frame that it did not cause
to quake; yea, it did pierce them to the very soul, and did
cause their hearts to burn.

3 Nephi 11:6
And behold, the third time they did understand the voice
which they heard; and it said unto them:

A Risen Lord To All The World

3 Nephi 11:7
Behold my Beloved Son, in whom I am well pleased, in whom I have glorified my name - hear ye him.

3 Nephi 11:8
And it came to pass, as they understood they cast their eyes up again towards heaven; and behold, they saw a Man descending out of heaven; and he was clothed in a white robe; and he came down and stood in the midst of them; and the eyes of the whole multitude were turned upon him, and they durst not open their mouths, even one to another, and wist not what it meant, for they thought it was an angel that had appeared unto them.

3 Nephi 11:9
And it came to pass that he stretched forth his hand and spake unto the people, saying:

3 Nephi 11:10
Behold, I am Jesus Christ, whom the prophets testified shall come into the world.

3 Nephi 11:11
And behold, I am the light and the life of the world; and I have drunk out of that bitter cup which the Father hath given me, and have glorified the Father in taking upon me the sins of the world, in the which I have suffered the will of the Father in all things from the beginning.

A Risen Lord To All The World

Americas

3 Nephi 11:12
And it came to pass that when Jesus had spoken these words the whole multitude fell to the earth; for they remembered that it had been prophesied among them that Christ should show himself unto them after his ascension into heaven.

3 Nephi 11:16
And when they had all gone forth and had witnessed for themselves, they did cry out with one accord, saying:

3 Nephi 11:17
Hosanna! Blessed be the name of the Most High God! And they did fall down at the feet of Jesus, and did worship him.

THE PURPOSE OF HIS COMING

Luke 19:10
For the Son of man is come to seek and to save that which was lost.

John 10:10
The thief cometh not, but for to steal, and to kill, and to destroy: I am come that they might have life, and that they might have it more abundantly.

John 10:11
I am the good shepherd: the good shepherd giveth his life for the sheep.

2 Nephi 2:6
Wherefore, redemption cometh in and through the Holy Messiah; for he is full of grace and truth.

2 Nephi 2:7
Behold, he offereth himself a sacrifice for sin, to answer the ends of the law, unto all those who have a broken heart and a contrite spirit; and unto none else can the ends of the law be answered.

The Purpose of His Coming

Mosiah 16:9
He is the light and the life of the world; yea, a light that is endless, that can never be darkened; yea, and also a life which is endless, that there can be no more death.

Mosiah 16:10
Even this mortal shall put on immortality, and this corruption shall put on incorruption, and shall be brought to stand before the bar of God, to be judged of him according to their works whether they be good or whether they be evil -

Mosiah 16:11
If they be good, to the resurrection of endless life and happiness; and if they be evil, to the resurrection of endless damnation, being delivered up to the devil, who hath subjected them, which is damnation -

Mosiah 3:11
For behold, and also his blood atoneth for the sins of those who have fallen by the transgression of Adam, who have died not knowing the will of God concerning them, or who have ignorantly sinned.

Our Closing Witness

John 11:25
Jesus said unto her, I am the resurrection, and the life: he
that believeth in me, though he were dead, yet shall he
live:

Acts 4:12
Neither is there salvation in any other: for there is none
other name under heaven given among men, whereby we
must be saved.

2 Nephi 25:26
And we talk of Christ, we rejoice in Christ, we preach of
Christ, we prophesy of Christ, and we write according to
our prophecies, that our children may know to what
source they may look for a remission of their sins.

Moroni 10:31
And awake, and arise from the dust, O Jerusalem; yea,
and put on thy beautiful garments, O daughter of Zion;
and strengthen thy stakes and enlarge thy borders forever,
that thou mayest no more be confounded, that the
covenants of the Eternal Father which he hath made unto
thee, O house of Israel, may be fulfilled.

ABOUT THE AUTHORS

After publishing Behold, A Savior Is Born, we felt impressed to create a companion volume focused on Easter. The birth of the Savior is a miracle, but His willing sacrifice and Resurrection are the reason He came.

As we searched the scriptures, we were again reminded that the story of Jesus Christ is woven across many books of holy writ—from the premortal councils of heaven to the empty tomb. This book gathers those verses into one place, allowing the story of His life, sacrifice, and victory over death to be read as one unified witness.

Our hope is that it can be read throughout the days leading up to Easter and the Passover, inviting families to gather, read, and center their hearts on Jesus Christ.

Natalie and Jonathan have been married for over twenty-five years and are the parents of two children. Both are creators who find joy in serving and uplifting others. Natalie is an interior and architectural designer and the creator of a motivational podcast focused on wellbeing and healing, inspired by her journey through chronic illness. She serves actively in her church and community. Jonathan is a middle school teacher, coach, and author of more than twenty children's books, with a passion for motivating and encouraging youth.